Youth Futsal Skills and Strategies

A Guide for Players, Coaches, and Parents

Jeff Raymer

Illustrated by Bence Balaton

Cover design by Mala Baranove

Copyright © 2013 by Jeff Raymer

All rights reserved.

ISBN: 1494811782

ISBN-13: 978-1494811785

Dedication

To the Purple People Eaters, the Blue Sharks, the Man-Eating Oranges, and the Green Gators

Contents

Why Futsal? 1

The Basics 5

1 v 1 Offense 9

1 v 1 Defense 17

1 v 1 Practice Method 21

2 v 2 Offense 23

2 v 2 Defense 31

2 v 2 Practice Method 33

3 v 3 Offense 35

3 v 3 Defense 39

3 v 3 Practice Method 41

4 v 4 and 5 v 5 43

Parts of the Game 47

Unbalanced Sides 49

Game Situations 53

Goalkeeper Play 65

Some Fun Developmental Games 71

Coaching Responsibilities 79

Parent's Responsibilities 87

Why Futsal?

Basketball has five players per side. Volleyball has six per side. Baseball has nine. Football and soccer teams each field eleven players at a time. Each sport has its unique rules and strategies.

Unfortunately, turning 22 young players loose on a soccer field, each with a limited understanding of positions and responsibilities, can degenerate the game into a swarm of kids chasing the ball. Some kids remain on the outer fringes of the swirling tornado of children, rarely getting into the action, while a few of the more aggressive kids dominate the action. Eventually one player will break free with the ball from the tangle of children, and the rest will engage in hot pursuit. The cycle continues until the ball either goes out of bounds or into the goal, possibly the right goal.

The reality with the youngest of athletes is that rather than one team of eleven players against another team of eleven players, the game can devolve into a multitude of separate one-versus-one games. With 22 players on the field, that's 231 possible combinations of one-versus-one games, including the possibility of teammates battling each other for the ball. While it may be exercise, and it may be fun, it isn't really soccer.

Of course, the governing bodies of soccer in the United States realized long ago that 11-versus-11 games did not benefit the development of young athletes. They agreed upon small-sided games in practice and in competition. Smaller teams means more touches and more involvement for each player. More involvement allows for more decision making opportunities, which ultimately leads to improved player development. This is good for the game of soccer in general.

Smaller is better, but what is the right size for soccer? One-versus-one is not practical for organized competition because there would need to be many more fields, more coaches, and more referees. Two-versus-two is better, but while two players can form a line, they cannot form a shape. In other words, two players can either be wide or they can be deep, but they cannot be both wide and deep at the same time unless they play on extreme diagonal opposite ends and opposite sides of the field, making gameplay almost impossible.

Three players is the minimum necessary to form a shape, in this case a triangle. Is three enough though? With three players we can talk about directions such as front and back, left and right. Without getting things out of balance though, it is difficult to talk about the middle with just three players per side. You can speak about the middle left-to-right, but not the middle front-to-back, at least not at the same time. Start talking about the middle front-to-back with three players, and now your shape is no longer balanced left-to-right. A triangle can be symmetrical in one direction, but not in both directions simultaneously.

For soccer development, four seems to be the optimum number of field players. Think of a diamond shape. It is balanced front to back and left to right. You can talk about middle both left-to-right, and middle front-to-back. This shape can at the same time have width, depth, and balance. Within this shape players can learn responsibilities, they have opportunities for more touches, and they have frequent ability to make decisions. For this reason, four-versus-four is the ultimate soccer development formation.

What about goalkeeping? In all of this talk of shapes we haven't considered goalkeepers. Of course soccer teams need goalkeepers. It is an important skill to learn and a position that many young players enjoy playing. Proper goalkeeping technique must be developed. If the back player in your four player diamond is the goalkeeper, then your diamond is unable to move up and down the field. With this said, you'll need a fifth player to play behind the diamond as goalkeeper. Therefore, the ideal developmental approach to the game of soccer will have four field players and one goalkeeper per team.

If you're familiar with futsal at all, you will realize that what we have just described is indeed futsal. Futsal is a sport played with five players per team, four court players and one goalkeeper. Futsal is always played with five players per team, even at the professional and World Cup levels. By its nature, the team formation of futsal fits the developmental needs of young soccer players better than soccer itself does, with no modification required.

The fundamental strategy of futsal is the same as that of soccer: spread the field or court on offense, and collapse on defense. Individual players are responsible not to be out of position so that they can cover a particular area or help their teammates. Futsal also encourages quick decision-making due to the speed of the ball moving across the hard floor surface, the smaller dimensions of the court, and the game's four-second play-in rule.

Futsal is the ultimate game to teach responsibility, shape, and teamwork in a fast-paced decision-making environment. Since it is played indoors, the game allows for four full seasons of development because neither rain nor snow, nor hot nor cold, will stop the play.

What follows in this book, is an introduction to the game of futsal. Although we will give some occasional tips regarding patterns of play, our main emphasis will not be on formations or plays. Instead, we will emphasize fundamental skills and strategies. It is our philosophy that successful teams rely more on playmakers, and less on plays.

We also will not devote much effort to talking about futsal rules. Please download the FIFA Laws of the Game, and also review the rules of your specific league for complete information about the rules which apply to your match.

The Basics

The Court

Futsal is played indoors. Very few regulation futsal gyms are available in the United States. For this reason, most leagues will be using basketball gyms, modified for futsal use. In general, the typical basketball gym is smaller than preferred for futsal use, but it works. Each league may differ on how they utilize the basketball court's markings for areas of the futsal court. Leagues that play in the same gym season after season will likely lay down futsal-specific markings on the court.

If you're playing on an unmodified basketball court, you can use the three-point arc as the penalty area. The surface area is roughly the same as the futsal penalty area, although the basketball zone is not as wide, yet deeper, than the regulation futsal penalty zone.

The free throw line works almost perfectly for the penalty spot. Given that the court is shorter overall, the top of the key (where the free throw circle and three point arc intersect) is a reasonable secondary penalty spot. Alternatively, you could designate a second penalty spot halfway between the top of the key and the center circle. Notice in the diagram below how the regulation futsal second penalty spot is at this half-way distance naturally. We'll describe the use of the secondary penalty spot later, in the *Game Situations* chapter.

Simply put, just use what's available, make sure everyone is clear on what the markings represent, and play the game even if you don't have the ideal regulation futsal court.

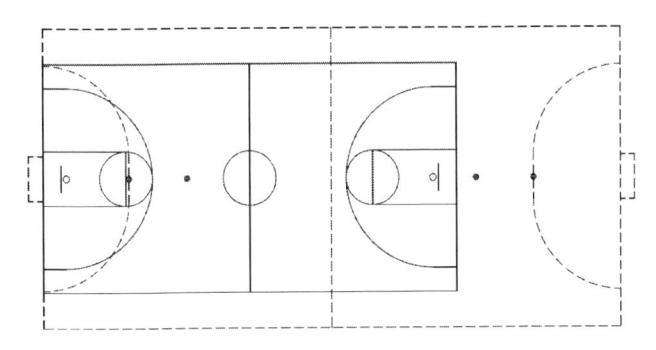

Figure 1: Comparison of Standard Futsal and Basketball Courts

The Ball

Perhaps the most important piece of equipment you can have for playing a futsal game is a proper ball. Do not use a regular soccer ball, even an indoor soccer ball. In order to properly play futsal, you should use a ball specifically designed for futsal use.

The futsal ball has less bounce and thereby less sensitivity. This feature is required when playing on the hard surface of a gym floor. Otherwise, the ball will be too fast, or too hot if you will. Using anything other than a futsal ball for futsal will only make the game frustrating, as most plays will end with the ball uncontrollably rolling out of bounds.

The Goal

Portable goals can be dangerous if not properly secured. Additionally, no one wants to stop play in order to chase the goal around the gym every time someone takes a shot on goal. If you are going to use a portable goal, make sure it is anchored properly per the manufacturer's instructions (sandbags and duct tape are commonly used for this purpose.) A nicely secured goal makes for a safe and quality futsal court.

Portable goals are not a necessity, however. In a pinch, strategically-placed cones can be used to mark the goals. The only downside is that balls played in the air are left up to interpretation as to whether they are within the goal or were played outside of it.

The Uniform

Comfortable clothing is required to play futsal, along with regular gym shoes and shin guards. Coaches should not allow players to play without shin guards; no exceptions! Remember, soccer socks go on the outside of the shin guards in order to keep the guard directly on top of the shin where it belongs.

Do not wear cleats, as they are designed for grass surfaces, not hard floors. While cleats provide good traction on the ground, they are incredibly slick on hard floor surfaces. Cleats could also damage the floor, causing the owner of the gym to cease to allow futsal games there.

Also remember, FIFA regulations state that no earrings or other jewelry are to be worn while playing soccer. This rule likewise applies to futsal.

Goalkeepers should wear a different colored jersey, or a practice penny over top of their jersey, in order to distinguish them from the four court players. Gloves are not necessary, and may in fact hinder the goalkeeper's performance, especially if the gloves do not fit properly. Most youth will find goalkeeper gloves to be too large for them. Goalkeepers are allowed to wear pants rather than shorts, and may choose to wear elbow and knee pads.

1 v 1 Offense

One-versus-one is the most basic sports situation, and many situations within a futsal match can be distilled down to 1 v 1 scenarios. Examples include a defender poking the ball away from a dribbler, or an offensive player protecting the ball from a defender long enough to make a pass to a teammate. All good players have good 1 v 1 skills. For this reason, futsal training should involve quite a bit of 1 v 1 specific training.

The one-versus-one offensive scenario involves either *protecting the ball* or *getting past an opponent*.

Protection, also called shielding, only works for a couple of seconds in a real game. Players must learn to keep their body between the ball and their opponent. If you try to shield for more than a couple of seconds in a real game, you'll be swarmed with defenders.

You can build your ball protection prowess using a practice shielding drill, turning your body as your partner tries to move around you to get the ball. Try using the sole of your foot to move the ball and keep it away from your partner. Using the sole to control the ball is a futsal specialty. Keep the ball away from your partner and don't move until you need to; allow your movements to be a response to your partner's attempts to get at the ball.

Figure 2: Partners Practicing the Shielding Drill

Getting past an opponent involves either a *change of direction* or a *change of speed*.

The first key to getting past an opponent is proper dribbling technique. The basic dribble involves raising your knee, turning your foot so that the toes point down toward the floor, and pushing the center of the ball (also called the sweet spot) with either your pinky toe or the knuckle of your big toe. Be able to use either, but the pinky will probably give you a lighter touch, which is especially beneficial in futsal.

Figure 3: Dribbling with the Pinky Toe

Figure 4: Dribbling with the Knuckle of the Big Toe

Use a gentle touch and keep the ball close enough so that there is no step with the kicking foot in between touches with the ball. For example, if you're dribbling with your right foot, your stepping pattern should be: **push right**, step left, **push right**, step left, **push right**, and so on. If you're dribbling with the ball too far away, you're likely to get it poked away. You're kicking the ball too far away if you find yourself doing a pattern more like: **kick right**, step left, step right, step left, **kick right**, step left, step right, step left, **kick right**, and so on.

Being able to dribble with either foot gives you more options and makes you harder to defend. Practice the basic dribble using both your right foot and your left foot. Be able to slow down and speed up at will. These *speed changes* will help you get past an opponent. You'll lull your opponent to sleep with your slow dribbling, then speed up to accelerate past them.

A trick which will get you past your defender is to dribble fast, slow down for a few seconds to draw them in close to you, then accelerate past them at the exact moment that they begin closing the distance and are moving toward you. It takes practice, but you can perfect it. This is Einstein's Theory of Relativity at its fundamental level. If they're still moving toward you at two miles per hour when you make your burst past them, and you're moving away from them at four miles per hour, it makes it seem like you're moving away from them at six miles per hour because of the complete opposite directions of motion at that split second. To them, you seem like you're moving faster than you actually are. It's all relative, but it makes you look like a superstar!

After you've learned to change your speed, you'll need to learn to *change direction* to get past a defender. Practice various moves and combinations using different surfaces of the foot. Use a soft touch and use slight angles close to the defender when changing direction rather than making large arcing movements around them. Be able to use the inside of the foot, the outside of the foot, or the sole of the foot to change direction.

When you are able to combine your changes of direction and your changes of speed, you will have perfected getting past a defender. Try combining a couple of moves together, but don't string too many moves together or you'll be spending too much time with the ball and the opponent is likely to poke it away from you. Use your moves efficiently.

Some sample 1-2 combinations are presented next. Remember, small angles work better than big movements. A soft touch and proper timing, combined with the right distance and protection from your opponent, is required in order to make these combinations work. The right time to execute a move is when you have the defender committed to going a particular direction, perhaps as the result of a fake move you've made in that direction. Although we present these moves using the right foot as an example, remember to practice using both feet in order to be able to use these moves to go either direction.

Outside-Inside: Fake right with a light bump with the outside of the right foot, then scoop the ball back left with the inside of the right foot. Now dribble away to the left. This also works by using the sole of the foot to move the ball: fake outside keeping the ball under the foot, then roll the ball inside while releasing it out from under the foot.

Figure 5: Getting Free Using the Outside-Inside Move

Inside-Inside: Fake left with a light bump with the inside of the right foot, then follow with a bump to the right using the inside of the left foot. Now dribble away to the right.

Figure 6: Getting Free Using the Inside-Inside Move

Inside-Outside: Fake left with a light bump with the inside of the right foot, then scoop the ball back right with the outside of the right foot. Now dribble away to the right. This also works by using the sole of the foot to move the ball: fake inside keeping the ball under the foot, then roll the ball outside while releasing it out from under the foot.

Figure 7: Getting Free Using the Inside-Outside Move

Youth Futsal Skills and Strategies

Another offensive maneuver, which is similar to a reverse dribble in basketball, combines protection with getting past an opponent. In this move, you approach an opponent straight on, but then turn your back to them while protecting the ball. You continue turning, keeping your back to the defender and the ball away from them, until you can dribble out on the other side away from their defense. You have to execute this move close to the defender, preferably with your back actually touching them, in order for it to be the most effective.

Once you're past your defender you'll likely either pass or shoot the ball. Like dribbling, you should practice shooting with both the left foot and the right foot. When you're close to the goal, you can often slip a shot in using either the inside or outside of your foot. In that case, you perform the shot in the same way that you would a pass. We'll cover passing in the next chapter. Target the lower corners of the goal since those shots are the most difficult for the goalkeeper to stop.

Figure 8: Always be ready to Shoot

Shots from further out on the floor require finely-tuned accuracy. In addition, you might choose to use a power shot. Much practice time is required in order to master the proper shooting technique. Don't spend time practicing on a stationary ball, since the ball is only stationary in the game of futsal at kickoff, kick-in, or penalty and free kick situations. The rest of the time, the ball is moving.

Practicing kicking with a stationary ball can lead to the common mistake of moving backward to get a running start at kicking the ball during a live game. To avoid this problem, and to make the practice more game-like, always perform shooting practice using a moving ball. At the minimum, bump the ball to get it rolling, then practice the shot.

The non-shooting foot, also called the plant leg because you plant it to the floor when you shoot, is the key to accuracy in shooting. The ball will go wherever the toes of that planted foot are pointed; so you want to make sure the toes of the planted leg are pointing straight at the target. Bring the shooting foot toward the ball with toes pointing down toward the floor. The flat top surface of the shooting foot, the area where your shoe laces zig-zag back and forth between your toes and where the laces tie, should contact the ball.

Figure 9: Preparing for the Shot with Plant Foot Targeting the Goal and Winding up the Kicking Foot

Striking the ball on the sweet spot, in other words directly at the middle top-to-bottom and middle left-to-right, while your head is pointed down will send the ball straight and low. Raising your head up and striking the ball slightly under the sweet spot will lift the ball off the floor. Players should be able to shoot low or high, and practice hitting the bottom and top corners of the goal.

Youth Futsal Skills and Strategies

Figure 10: Shooting Targets at the Corners of the Goal

The knee of the kicking foot raises, and the relaxed arms of the player swing across the body at the point of impact with the ball. You will actually break contact with the floor on the most powerful of shots, launching forward with the kick, landing again on the kicking foot, and continuing to step forward toward the goal. Do not strike the ball and then suddenly stop your forward momentum like you've ran into a brick wall. Doing that will reduce your power. Always follow through on your shot. Following through puts you in position to replay the shot in a rebound scenario, for example when the goalkeeper knocks the ball back toward you, or when the ball hits either an upright post or the horizontal bar of the goal and bounces back toward you.

Figure 11: The Follow-through after the Shot

1 v 1 Defense

The main rule of defense is: you can't stop everything, so give them what you want them to have. As an example, you can't always stop the ball from advancing up the court. With that said, choose not to give up the middle of the court. Instead, allow the ball to advance up the sides where it is less dangerous because it is more difficult to shoot a goal accurately from there.

You can effectively force the dribbler to the side by opening your defensive stance up to one side or the other, rather than playing with your back flat to the goal. For example, to force the dribbler to her or his left, you'll stand with your back to the goal line but with your right side closer to the goal line than your left side, opening yourself up at an angle. You're basically inviting the dribbler to go in the direction you want them to go.

Figure 12: Opening up the Defensive Stance to Invite the Dribbler to the Edge and Away from the Middle

Since most dribblers are right-footed, what we have just described is your preferred defensive stance. The dribbler will likely continue to dribble with his or her right foot, bringing the ball directly in front of you where it is easy for you to poke away. Even if they don't bring the ball in front of you, they'll dribble away from you with their left foot, but probably not as effectively as they can dribble with their right.

Forcing defenders to the side increases the chance that they will turn the ball over by dribbling it out of bounds. Do not be so bent on forcing them to their left that you drive them all the way across the court, passing through the middle in the process. Force them to whichever side is closer, even if it means allowing them to take the ball with their preferred dribbling foot. Even if you can't stop them, you've given them less room to work in and hopefully you have a teammate closing in behind you to offer help. We'll talk more about defensive help from your teammates later in the book.

Remember that playing 1 v 1 defense is not the same as playing goalkeeper. Your job in 1 v 1 defense is to get the ball away from the dribbler and then start playing your own offense and trying to score your own goal. Don't stay back and watch; instead, get on the ball.

The process for getting on the ball is to *start fast, finish slow, stay under control, don't stab,* and *be patient*. Most of all, don't give up a clear shot at the goal.

Start Fast: Once again, you are not a goalkeeper in the 1 v 1 practice scenario. Don't stay back and watch; instead, get on the ball. You must advance quickly to close the distance between yourself and the player with the ball. Travel along a line between the goal and the ball so as to not give a clear shot at the goal.

Finish Slow: As you're approaching the final few steps between you and the player with the ball, you'll need to slow down. If you keep moving toward them too fast they'll use Einstein's Theory of Relativity against you. Slow down and take the final few steps with caution.

Stay under Control: Staying balanced and on the balls of your feet rather than your heels will allow you to make quick moves in any direction.

Don't Stab: The most common defensive mistake is poking at the ball too soon, when the offensive player has either good control or protection. Premature stabbing at the ball will take you off-balance and allow the offensive player to make her or his move when you're at a disadvantage.

Be Patient: Wait for the right moment to poke the ball away from the offensive player. Look for the point when they dribble the ball close to you, when they dribble too far out in front of their own body, or when they're crossing the ball in front of themselves and trying to change direction. If you try to go too soon, you'll end up giving them an advantage because you'll be off-balance.

Of course there comes a time when the player you're defending is really close to your goal and patience must be weighed against the desperate need to stop the ball. At that time, you may need to take a gamble and just go for it. A defensive concept called *good, better, best* applies in this situation. It is *good* to kick the ball out of bounds to stop the play and allow your team to set up their defense. It is *better* to get the ball away from the opponent and kick it safely toward the goal you're trying to score into; perhaps your teammates can follow it up for a score. It is *best* to get the ball away from the opponent, control it yourself, and either safely dribble, pass, or shoot.

No matter how good of a defensive player you are, there are times when you'll get beat by a great change of speed or change of direction move. It is during those times that you must *recover*.

Recovery is the act of catching up to the offensive player and re-establishing a good defensive position on them. The key to good recovery is the route you take to catch up. Most importantly, don't follow their path. If you do, you'll be following them all the way until they score a goal. Instead, you must sacrifice covering the dribbler for a moment and make an all-out-effort run on a straight line toward the goal. You should have an advantage in this run because they'll be dribbling a ball and you will not. Run a sufficient distance past the offensive player, then turn and play defense on them again.

1 v 1 Practice Method

The 1 v 1 practice game is played side-to-side on the court. The reason for playing side-to-side rather than end-to-end is that you rarely have more than a few seconds of dribbling play at a time in a game. You don't want to overemphasize long dribbling runs that aren't feasible in game situations. This also allows two 1 v 1 games to be going on at the same time on the court, allowing a coach to use practice time and space more efficiently.

Stand in your own goal and serve the ball to your partner on the opposite end by passing them the ball. They try to score in the goal you were standing in. You try to score in the goal they were standing in. Get on them and try to recover the ball and score. This is not a goalkeeping drill. Be patient and look for the best shots, don't settle for booting long shots as soon as you get the ball. Use this practice time to work on your ball protection and offensive moves, to work on dribbling and shooting with either foot, and to work on closing in and executing your will defensively.

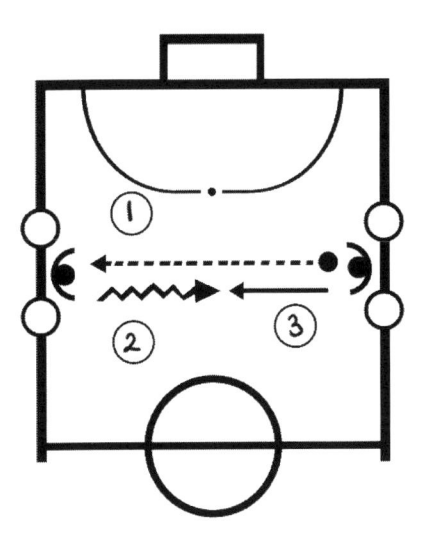

Figure 13: 1 v 1Practice Method

2 v 2 Offense

The movie poster for a 1977 science fiction movie declared, *"We are not alone."* Youth coaches must spend much of their time repeating to their players, *"You are not alone."* Offensively, futsal players must *recognize* their teammates, *communicate* with their teammates, *support* their teammates, and *encourage* their teammates.

Offensively, your teammate will *recognize* you if you are playing proper off-the-ball offense. Remember that the futsal strategy offensively is to spread the floor. Don't play too close to your teammate. Coming toward them only succeeds in bringing your defender to them in addition to the defender that is already on them. Establish a position away from your teammate, making it difficult for the defense to cover both of you at the same time.

In order to be recognized, however, you must not stand behind a defender. If there is a defender on a straight line between your partner and yourself, then your partner can't see you. If they can't see you, they can't pass to you. If you're not available for a pass, then you're not *supporting* your teammate.

Communication can be either verbal or non-verbal. Verbal communication should always be encouraged by the coaches. Players must talk to one another when playing on the court. Since futsal is not played in a library, talking is not only acceptable, it is necessary.

As players practice more together in 2 v 2 situations, they will learn the body actions of their teammates and non-verbal communication will be possible. Study your teammate so that you know her or his intentions. Perhaps a running player habitually slows down prior to breaking hard toward the goal. Be ready for it, and look to get them the pass. Perhaps a dribbling player has a great change of direction move and an opportunity will typically be available to receive a pass if you play ahead of them. Be ready for it, and look to receive the pass from them.

All of the players on a team must respect each other. It doesn't matter if they are friends at school or not, on the court they are teammates and team comes first before self. Everyone makes mistakes from time to time. It is part of the learning process. Teammates *encourage* each other when things don't go right. Coaches are not to allow a teammate to speak negatively or derogatorily about another teammate.

Passing

As previously mentioned, passing involves more than just the mechanics of passing. Playing in the proper position off the ball is an important part of being a good teammate. Wherever there are players saying, *"No one will pass me the ball,"* there are coaches saying, *"You were never playing in a position to receive a pass."*

Before playing against defense, work on passing with a partner. Don't stand across from each other and simply pass back-and-forth, instead move around the floor passing to each other.

When on the move, learn to pass ahead of your teammate; pass to where they are going rather than to where they are at. This is called leading the player with the pass. If you're both moving up the floor and you pass to where your partner is at, then if they keep moving, the pass will end up behind them. You don't want to make your partner stand and wait for a pass, or have to come back to receive a pass. Doing so will only lead to stolen passes once you have defense on the floor against you.

As you're playing the passing game with your partner, you'll pick up on non-verbal cues. Pay attention to how your partner moves. Look for times when the player without the ball is breaking toward the goal. Look for times when the player with the ball is looking up wanting to pass it off. Maintain eye contact between yourself and your partner.

A set play that you can practice with a partner is called the *give-and-go*. The *give-and-go* works in basketball as well as in futsal. Basically, one player makes the pass to the other player. This is the *Give*. Then the player who made the pass makes a cut toward the goal. This is the *Go*. This may be followed by another pass back to the original player, another *Give* if you will. It isn't called the *give-and-go-and-give* because even though the initial passer always *Goes*, the receiving player has the option of passing back or not, depending on how the defense responds in a game.

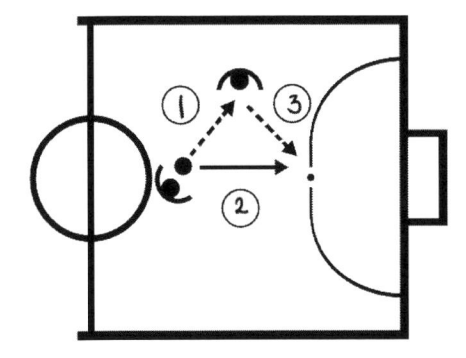

Figure 14: Give-and-go Play

Perfect your *give-and-go* by starting with two-touch passing back to the cutting player. Two-touch means you receive the pass with one touch, then pass back to them with a second touch. Eventually move to one-touch passing. One-touch passing means that you maneuver your body while the ball is coming toward you such that you can send the pass back to the cutting player with a single quick, but soft and accurate, touch.

Another fun two-player set play to practice is one that you'll want to develop a hand signal or verbal cue for. You can call it the Charlie Brown Play. Player One shields the ball from a defender, controlling the ball under his or her foot away from the defender. Player Two runs around the outside of the player controlling the ball and shoots the ball being held by Player One toward the goal. This violates the concept of not bringing your defender toward the other player, but it is a fun trick play to try once a game or so.

Before we discuss proper passing mechanics, let's discuss the opportunity for fancy passes in futsal. Futsal players are among the most skilled athletes in regard to ball control. We'll discuss juggling later in the book, but enough dribbling and juggling practice will allow you to make fantastic dribbles and passes on the court. With your coach's permission, consider using a portion of your two-player practice time as a chance to try out behind-the-leg passes to a partner beside you, and no-look passes to a partner behind you. Use these with caution in a game and not until they have been practiced in two-player practice so that both partners know what is going to happen. Even the most talented professional futsal players only use these moves sparingly in the 5 v 5 game, as an occasional surprise move.

Figure 15: A Behind-the-leg Pass

Finally, we'll end this chapter by discussing proper passing mechanics. As in shooting, the opposite foot to the passing foot is the key to accurate passing. Again, we'll call this the plant foot. The toes of the plant foot should face the intended target.

Figure 16: Target the Pass with the Planted Foot and Swing the Passing Leg toward the Ball

The passing leg swings toward the target and the inside of the foot makes contact with the ball. The arch of the foot hugs the ball when contact is made. As in shooting, keeping your head down and contacting the ball on the sweet spot will keep the pass low to the floor. Raising your head and contacting the ball below the sweet spot will lift the ball into the air. Remember to lead your partner and pass to where they're moving rather than to where they're at.

Figure 17: Use the Inside of the Foot for Passing

Figure 18: The Follow-through after the Pass

Passing with the inside of the foot is the safest and most accurate method of passing. You may also execute a flick pass with the outside of the foot. This is often a quick decision, perhaps in tight quarters or in a fast break scenario.

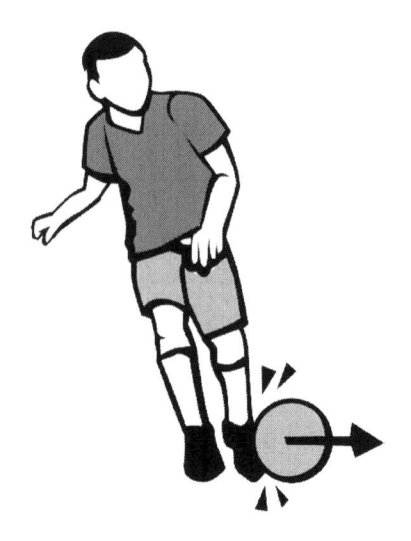

Figure 19: A Flick Pass with the Side of the Foot during a Fast Break

Speaking of fast breaks, this is perhaps the right time to start discussing this concept. As in basketball, the fast break is a viable scoring option in futsal. Unlike soccer, there is no offside rule in futsal. The lack of an offside rule makes the fast break even more viable for scoring in futsal than in soccer.

In the game of futsal your team is always in one of three states: (1) your team has possession of the ball and is playing offense, (2) the other team has possession of the ball and your team is playing defense, or (3) possession is changing from one team to the other. Possession can change as the result of a score, a missed shot, a ball kicked out of bounds, or a steal (also called a tackle in soccer and futsal, although we avoid using this term in the U.S. because it is often confused due to American football and implies excessive physical contact.)

To facilitate the fast break in a 2 v 2 game, watch for a change of possession when your teammate has won possession of the ball. In that scenario, release toward the opposite goal and create a passing angle such that your teammate can send you a long pass up the floor. You'll need to watch your teammate, however, and will need to come back to offer support via an outlet pass if they are pressured and can't get the ball ahead to you.

2 v 2 Defense

Before playing 2 v 2, coaches should introduce two-player defense with some half-court 1 v 2 drills. One player will have the ball and be covered by two defenders. Rather than swarming the ball and double-teaming, however, the two defenders will use the drill to learn to cover the ball using *ball* and *help* positions. One player will play aggressively on the *ball* just as in 1 v 1 defense, while the other player will take a *help* position situated between the on-ball defender and the goal.

The *help* position is in place for when the offensive player makes an incredible change of direction or speed and gets past the on-ball defender. The *help* defender then races to become the on-ball defender, and the player that was beat recovers and takes the place of the *help* defender. Verbal communication is extremely important in this case, as the two defenders must be fluent while changing from playing on the *ball* to playing *help*.

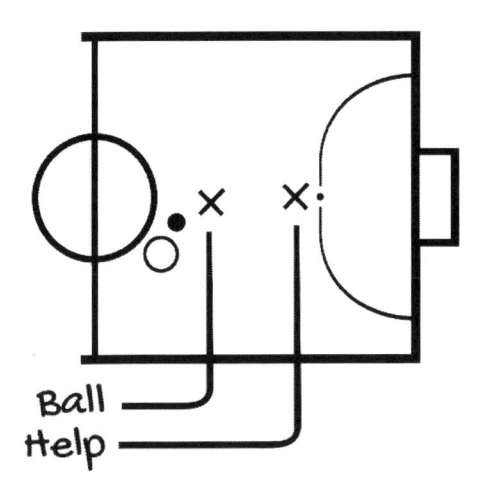

Figure 20: 1 v 2 Defense

After players learn the *ball* and *help* positions through sufficient repetitions in the 1 v 2 drill, play can progress to 2 v 2. This adds complexity, because the *help* player can no longer be completely preoccupied with staying between the partner and the goal, otherwise they'll leave the second offensive player unguarded for wide open looks at the goal.

Youth Futsal Skills and Strategies

In the 2 v 2 game, the off-ball defender learns to stay in a position to offer *help*, but not to completely leave the player she or he is responsible for. When *help* is required, the *help* defender switches off his or her own player, and the defender who was beaten must recover to be able to play the other offensive player, while in-turn offering *help* if needed.

2 v 2 Practice Method

Similar to the 1 v 1 practice game, the 2 v 2 practice game is played side-to-side on the court. This allows for quick action. The team starting with the ball positions two players side-by-side in the middle of the court. Play begins when one of these two players kicks a gentle kick-off to her or his partner.

The defense begins by standing side-by-side a sufficient distance from the kick-off team, ready to defend. The two defensive players should constantly communicate who is on the ball and who is playing help. These roles will change continually as the ball is passed around.

This practice game allows the teams to practice the three states of the game as offense will change to defense, and back again quickly. Learn when to release on the fast break and when to stay back in support of your teammate.

Offensively work on spreading the floor, on quick accurate passing, and on the give-and-go. Defensively, do not give up the middle of the floor, but force play to the side.

3 v 3 Offense

With three players, you can really start to spread the full width of the floor on offense. A player can play in the middle, and one on each side. This is called playing the lanes, or filling the lanes. There are three lanes: a left lane, a middle lane, and a right lane. For balance with three players, each lane should contain one player on offense.

Utilize the far edges of the court and learn to control the ball near these edges. At high levels of play, a lot of action occurs along the edges, keeping the center open for a quick pass and scoring opportunity. At the youth level, a lot of balls will go out of bounds while players are learning to keep the ball in play along the edges. Patience is the key, as players develop the soft touch required to keep the ball in-bounds.

Also with three players, a team can begin thinking about shape offensively. The shape you're looking for is a triangle. With a triangle, you can have one player back and two players forward. Alternatively, you can have two players back and one player forward.

In order to make things tougher on the defense, the triangle should not be stationary. Instead, there should be a lot of movement both with and without the ball. Youth coaches will tell their players not to stand still, or will tell them to move around. Without some additional directions, however, the movement can become random purposeless movement such as running in circles or running toward the ball. With a 3 v 3 offense, we propose three scenarios: *flipping the triangle, inverting the triangle,* and *rotating the triangle*.

Flipping the Triangle: If a player passes from the right side back to the middle, for example, she or he will then cut to the goal looking for a return pass. This is the give-and-go move previously discussed. If the return pass doesn't come, then rather than going back to the right lane, the player will continue over to the left lane. Now there are two players in the left lane, making it unbalanced. To balance the floor, the player who was already in the left lane will run across the floor to the right lane, going through the middle, looking to receive a pass on the way through. This movement creates potential passing and shooting opportunities if the defense doesn't respond.

Youth Futsal Skills and Strategies

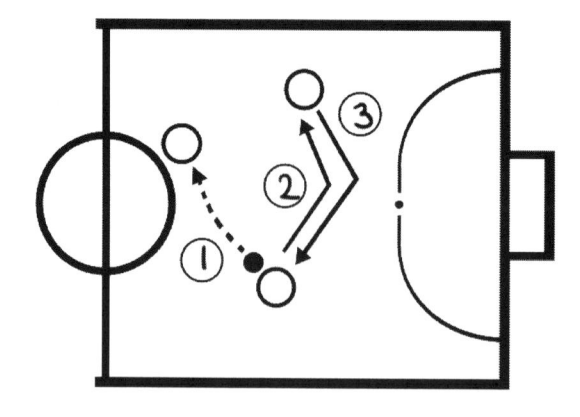

Figure 21: Flipping the Triangle

Inverting the Triangle: If the middle back player passes ahead to one of the sides of the triangle, then she or he will run forward toward the goal, following the give-and-go principle. This inverts the triangle because now two players are back, and one forward. Remember, there is no offside rule in futsal, so don't be afraid to send the ball forward to the cutting player. Make sure the cut toward the goal is purposeful, intended to get past the defender in order to receive a return pass and score a goal. The defender may have turned his or her head to watch the pass, in which case a backdoor cut is in order. If the defender is still playing strong, a change-of-direction or roll may get the cutting player free.

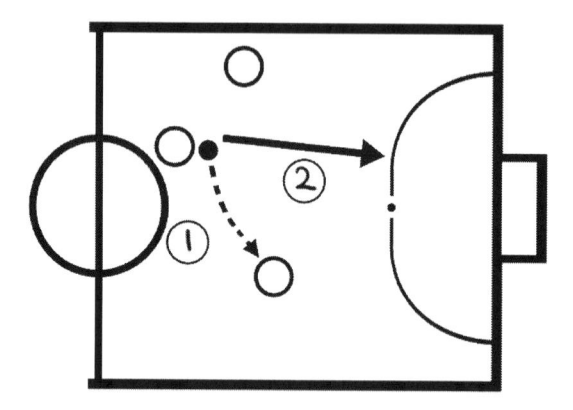

Figure 22: Inverting the Triangle

Rotating the Triangle: A final option with the triangle is turning, or rotating, the triangle. For example, if the right side player dribbles toward the back middle player, then the middle player is pushed to the left lane, and the left player is pulled across the court over to the right lane.

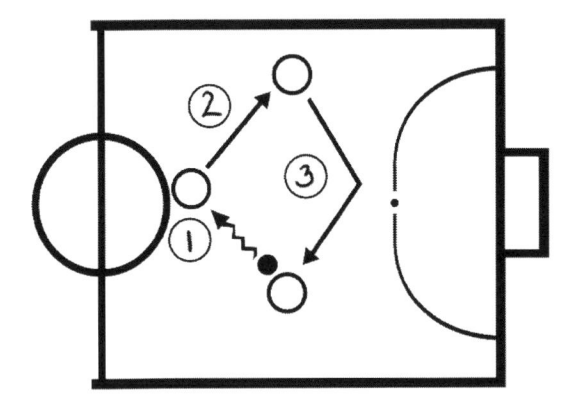

Figure 23: Rotating the Triangle

It has already been said, but is worth repeating: always be ready to shoot. A lot of long shots are taken in a futsal match. These shots result from passing the ball around until an opening presents itself. Everyone on offense must be ready to take advantage of the opportunity when it arrives.

Figure 24: Always be ready to Shoot

3 v 3 Defense

Coaches should begin teaching three-player defense by giving the defensive team an advantage. Begin with half-court 2 v 3 drills, with the two players having the ball and trying to score on the three players. With three defenders, this is the first opportunity a coach has to teach the *ball*, *help*, and *balance* positions. Rather than the three defenders swarming onto the ball, the purpose of this drill is to add the concept of *balance* to the player's defensive toolkit.

As in the 1 v 2 defensive drill, communication is vital. Whoever is closest to a player receiving a pass should assume an on-ball defensive position. They should call out something like, *"I have the ball."* Whoever is closest to the second offensive player should *balance* the floor by protecting against the pass. The remaining defensive player should position himself or herself between the on-ball defender and the goal to provide *help* in case it is needed.

During this drill, each player must understand that the concepts of *ball*, *help*, and *balance* are dynamic positions. It is not like a point guard in basketball, or a center or quarterback in American football. Depending on where the ball is passed, any particular player might be on the ball, or helping, or guarding against the pass.

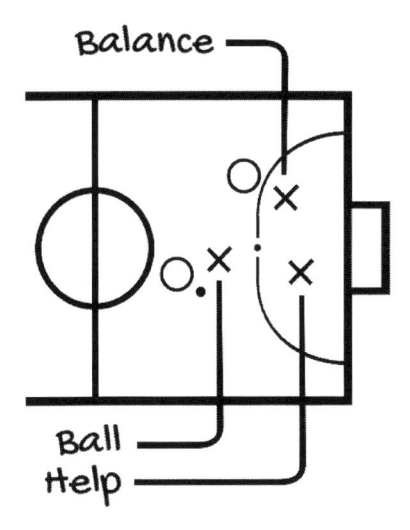

Figure 25: 2 v 3 Defense

Once the third offensive player is added and this becomes real 3 v 3 play, the concepts do not vanish, but distinguishing the help opportunity becomes more difficult. It is easy for players to drift into playing denial man-to-man defense. It is common for one player to be on the *ball* and the other two players engaged in a pass-denial *balance* role. Each of these other two players, however, must be ready to *help* should the on-ball defender be beaten. This concept is called sagging man-to-man defense.

When the ball is on one side of the court, the player guarding the player on the far opposite side is the natural player to assume a *help* role since he or she has time to recover and get back on the ball should a long pass be made across the court.

Every effort should be made to defensively keep the ball out of the middle of the floor since the middle offensive player can pass to either the right or left side. With two options, no help is available, making the middle player a dangerous triple threat, able to dribble, pass, or shoot.

3 v 3 Practice Method

3 v 3 features enough players to play the full length of the court. Playing side-to-side across the court will be too crowded. The team starting with the ball positions two players side by side in the middle of the court. Play begins when one of these two players kicks a gentle kick-off to her or his partner. The coach will likely suggest that the next kick after the initial short kick is a pass backward in order to establish possession and get into a wide triangle shape to control the ball and move it around on offense.

The defense begins by standing side-by-side a sufficient distance from the kick-off team, ready to defend. Each player should match up with someone and basically play man-to-man with the concepts of *ball*, *help*, and *balance* enforced.

The offense should continually work to control the ball and spread the floor. Fast breaking should be encouraged whenever change of possession occurs.

The on-ball defender should play tight, trying to recover the ball. Defenders on players without the ball must know where the ball is, and also know where their assigned player is. The off-ball defenders should sag off their assigned player enough to keep the ball out of the middle of the floor and be able to offer help, yet stay close enough to intercept a pass.

4 v 4 and 5 v 5

With 4 v 4 play, all field players are incorporated. Additionally, 5 v 5 play also includes the goalkeeper. Note that the goalkeeper could play at any level prior to 5 v 5 as well. If you want to play 1 v 1 plus goalkeepers, that's fine. The more game action that goalkeepers get, the better they'll develop.

With four players, each of the three lanes are filled. In addition, one lane will include two players. The typical four-player diamond shape has two players in the middle lane, one front and one back, but a coach might decide to play a triangle-and-one rather than a diamond. In a triangle-and-one, the front player will typically play on either the ball side, or the opposite side, depending on the coach's preference. A ball-side triangle-and-one can be used for additional give-and-go opportunities. The opposite-side option provides a passing outlet after dribble penetration.

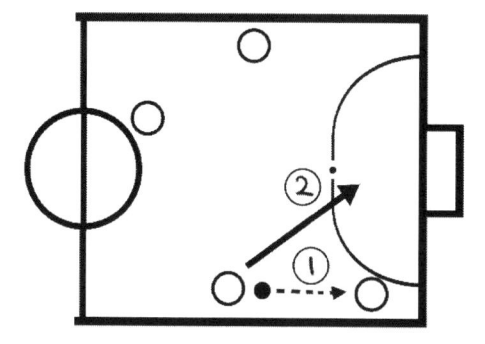

Figure 26: Ball-side Triangle-and-one Offense

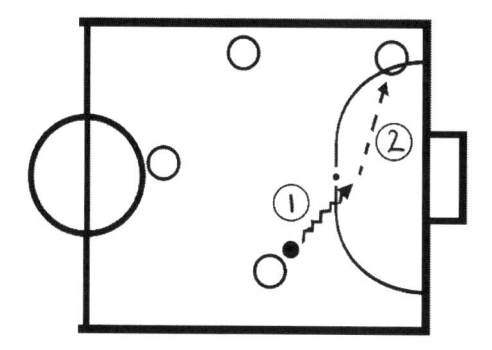

Figure 27: Opposite-side Triangle-and-one Offense

As in 3 v 3, the field players in 4 v 4 should interchange positions rather than being statically fixed in one corner of the diamond, or in one position of the triangle-and-one.

Just like the triangle, the diamond can be flipped through a give-and-go after a pass comes from the outside lane to the middle lane. Just like the triangle, the diamond can be rotated by dribbling from one corner to the other, pushing and pulling the other players accordingly.

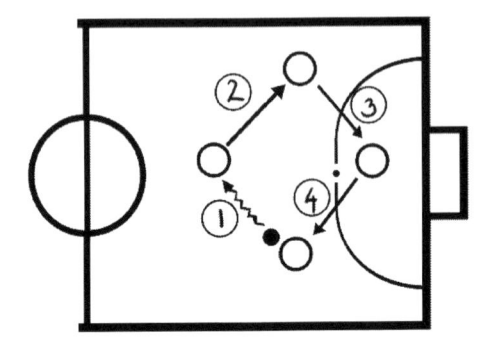

Figure 28: Rotating the Diamond

Both the diamond and triangle-and-one shapes are perfect for allowing movement both on and off the ball. As an example, consider a pass from the back middle to one of the side lanes. Using a give-and-go approach, the passer then cuts up the middle toward the goal. Seeing his teammate approaching, the player at the front middle position moves toward the side opposite the ball, thereby pushing the player in that position to the back of the diamond.

Defensively, all of the lessons previously learned still apply. A team might emphasize either protecting the goal, or recovering the ball. Since there are now four players available, a team might emphasize trapping the player with the ball by swarming a second player at the ball. Even when sending a second player to the ball, there are still two additional defensive field players available. One can be available to offer help, the other to provide balance against the passing attack. To confuse the opposing team, a coach might decide to alternate and occasionally play an aggressive swarming defense, and occasionally play a compressed protection style.

Within the 5 v 5 game, the team can practice *flying* the keeper. This simply means bringing the keeper forward away from the goal and playing her or him as a fifth field player. The keeper, of course, must use her or his feet rather than hands to control the ball outside the penalty area.

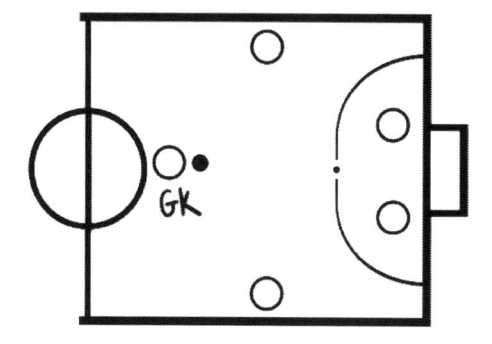

Figure 29: Flying the Keeper

The keeper should not come too far forward, always playing as the back player in the formation. *Flying* the keeper allows the offensive team to be more aggressive when looking for scoring opportunities. The team could play the goalkeeper at the back, a field player wide left, a field player wide right, and two field players forward toward the goal. Remember, there is no offside rule in futsal, so sending two field players ahead can result in fast break opportunities and put a lot of pressure on the defense.

Parts of the Game

It is possible for a team to improve a certain aspect of their game by isolating that part of the game in practice. The aspects of the game that can be isolated include *controlling the backcourt, controlling the middle of the court*, and *controlling the frontcourt*.

Controlling the Backcourt: Controlling the backcourt includes *protecting the goal*, and *dribbling out of the back*. In order to isolate and improve this aspect of the game, teams can divide the court in half and only work in one half of the court at a time. Using cones, increase the width of the goal in order to create a sense of urgency in *protecting the goal*. Additionally, create two small goals at opposite sides of the mid-court stripe to serve as targets for *dribbling the ball out of the backcourt*. One team will seek to score into the large goal, the other to pass to the sides and dribble through one of the small goals. Look for opportunities to cross the ball through the middle and quickly to the opposite side. Although this game works with as small as 2 v 2, the ideal size is 3 v 3. You may want to play without a goalkeeper in order to highly emphasize protection of the large goal by the field players.

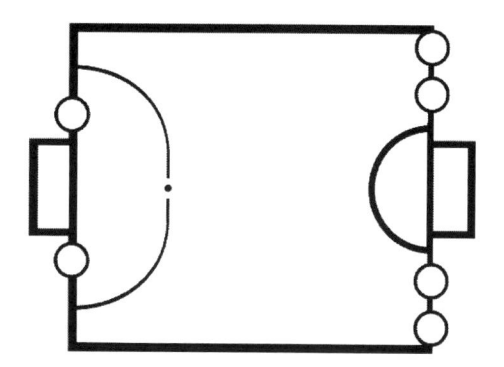

Figure 30: Controlling the Backcourt Practice Setup

Controlling the Middle of the Court: Use one half of the court to represent the center section of the court. One team will pass the ball around. This team scores one point with each successfully completed pass. The other team needs to recover the ball, and scores by dribbling across one of the end lines of the playing court. That team might need to make a couple of passes to get the ball to someone who can dribble across the line. For that team, however, those passes do not count as points; only the act of dribbling the ball across one of the end lines counts as a point. Once a team has successfully dribbled the ball out, the teams switch roles. Now the team which dribbled out becomes the team that scores points by completing successful passes. Keep in mind that booting the ball over the line is not the same as dribbling, and should not be counted as a successful point. Dribbling requires maintaining possession. In order to complete more successful passes, you might designate one player to play as a *neutral* player, open to receive passes from either team, but who does not attempt to defend.

Controlling the Frontcourt: A similar game to that used to improve controlling the backcourt can be used to improve controlling the frontcourt. Goals are placed at each end of the half court. One goal has a goalkeeper and one does not. The attacking team seeks to control the ball and score into the goal which contains a goalkeeper. Since there is a keeper in the goal, this team must pass around and find the open shot. The defending team scores by recovering the ball and sending it through the goal on the opposite end, the goal without a keeper. This simulates passing the ball out of the backcourt. Since scoring in this goal is easier, the pressure is on the offense to control the ball, keep it safe from the defense, and look for the best scoring opportunity.

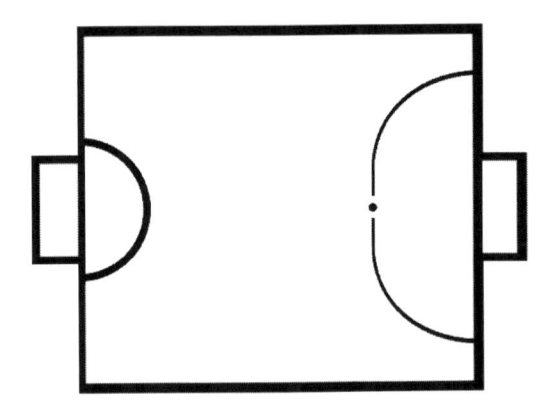

Figure 31: Controlling the Frontcourt Practice Setup

Unbalanced Sides

Sometimes playing with odd sides is necessary just because you don't have the right number of players. When this is the case, use the situation to encourage each team to learn a specific skillset or trait. Also, playing with odd sides intentionally is a way for coaches to provide opportunities to practice situations where one side has an advantage, or a disadvantage.

As an example, playing 2 v 3 full court gives one team an advantage on both offense and defense. The team with the advantage must learn to recognize and take advantage of this opportunity. Are the numbers in your favor? On offense, spread the floor, use quick passing, and attack the goal. Use your extra player to release up the court for fast break opportunities. On defense, use your numbers to double-team, swarm the ball, and regain control.

In a game situation, your advantage may only last for a few seconds, so you must learn to recognize and take advantage of it. Additionally, in a game situation not everyone will recognize the advantage immediately. As such, players must learn to communicate. Use verbal cues in practice such as *"we have an advantage"* so that these same cues can be used by the players in a live game situation.

Similarly, playing down a player can be used to encourage hustle play or ball protection by the disadvantaged team. Return to the fundamentals when numbers are not in your favor. You may not be able to stop everything, but what are you going to allow the team with the advantage to do? You may need to give up the edges of the court in order to protect the middle. All hope is not lost. Slow down the ball, be conservative rather than overly-aggressive, and look for the carefully timed play. Proper line of sight, movement without the ball, and quick passing is crucial offensively to the disadvantaged team.

After the coach has built up to full 5 v 5 games, she or he should still go back to the smaller-sided games in order to teach important fundamentals that are observed during games to need further work. You can pit any number of offensive players against any number of defensive players. If the defense has the numerical advantage, the coach dictates how they are to play; for example by practicing the *ball*, *help*, and *balance* roles. Defensive teams with an advantage could simply triple-team the ball, but the coach should specify the purpose of the training exercise both offensively and defensively.

The following chart shows some of the concepts that can be trained for particular numbers of players both offensively and defensively. Regardless of the number of players, offensive teams should always be ready to take advantage of shot openings with either foot. Also, you don't have to wait until 5 v 5 to start playing with goalkeepers. Any game, even a 1 v 1 game, could have goalkeepers in addition to the field players.

Number of Players	Offensive Concepts	Defensive Concepts
1	Ball protection, use of either foot, getting free using change of speed or direction, shooting, dribbling creativity	Getting on the ball, limiting offensive options, stopping the shot, winning the ball back, recovering when beaten
2	Positioning without the ball, communication, passing, fast breaking, give-and-go movement after passing, passing creativity	Aware and fluid positioning, communication, tight on-the-ball defense, sagging off-the-ball help defense
3	Width and balance in the lanes, triangular shape, passing for ball control, passing for open shots, flipping the triangle, inverting the triangle, rotating the triangle	Aware and fluid positioning, communication, tight on-the-ball defense, sagging off-the-ball help and balance defense
4	Width and depth, diamond shape, passing for ball control, passing for open shots, fast breaking, movement without the ball	Aware and fluid positioning, alternate aggressive trapping defense and compressed goal protection defense
5	Using the goalkeeper as an outlet to retain possession, or *flying* the keeper to apply additional scoring pressure	Same as 4 v 4 for field players, includes goalkeeper play (but a goalkeeper can be added as an additional player to any of the other levels from 1 v 1 to 3 v 3)

Game Situations

Coaches must make time to practice each of these special situations so that players know exactly what their responsibilities are in each scenario.

Kickoff

Just like soccer, you'll start each half of a futsal game with a kickoff. Likewise, there will also be a kickoff after each score. Like soccer, the kicking player may not touch the ball again until another player has touched it. In other words, a player may not simply start dribbling the ball rather than kicking it off.

If you watch youth soccer games, you may notice a large number of attempts to boot the ball as hard as possible into the goal on the initial kick. This strategy is strikingly absent from most levels of play higher than youth leagues. Booting the ball forward more likely than not results in handing the ball directly over to the other team. Furthermore, a goal may not be scored direct from a kickoff in futsal. The chances are slim of the ball glancing off a defender and into the goal; so an initial hard boot is not a logical approach to kicking off in futsal.

Most levels of play utilize a strategy that calls for a very short kickoff with two players close together, so as to emphasize maintaining possession after the kickoff. A common strategy is actually that after an initial kick forward of only a few inches, the kickoff team will actually pass the ball backward in order to settle into a pattern, maintain control, and spread the defense, before attacking the goal.

Regardless of strategy, a team must know how to line up against a kickoff just in case the opposing team attempts a quick score. Even if the first player doesn't boot the ball hard toward the goal on the initial kick, the second player might. The goalkeeper should have vision of the play, and defenders should line up such that there is not an unobstructed path from the ball to the goal. Think of the court like a foosball table, with the players serving as the obstructions, keeping the ball from going into the goal. Defensively, you want the ball to have to bounce off of your team before it reaches the goal.

Youth Futsal Skills and Strategies

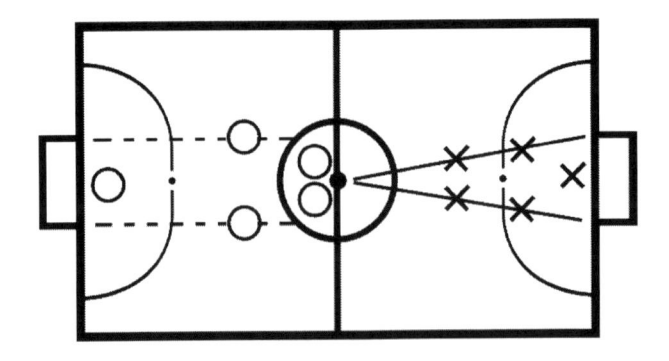

Figure 32: Kickoff Situation

The defense should compress and block the path to the goal. The defensive formation has no need to be wider than the goal. Consider reaction time and the angle of the ball coming off the kicker's foot when deciding upon a kick-off defensive formation. Players closer to the kicker will not have much reaction time to a quick hit, and therefore will not have time to cover much distance. The players behind them will have a bit more reaction time and can cover the increased distance required in this position. Finally, the goalkeeper has the longest reaction time and can cover the full width of the goal.

Kick In

When the ball crosses the sideline fully, the team that did not touch the ball last will have four seconds to kick it back in play. Pay close attention to the words *"when the ball crosses the sideline fully."* The ball touching the line is not considered out of bounds. The ball must be all the way across.

Futsal is a fast-paced game and sometimes the referees will get it right, sometimes they'll get it wrong. The important thing is to let them make the call. Don't stop playing until the whistle is blown; the ball may not be completely across the line from the referee's angle of sight. An additional and unique out of bounds rule for futsal is that the ceiling is also considered out of bounds, and a ball touching the ceiling will be played back in the same way as a ball crossing the sideline.

Use as much of your four seconds as necessary. Youth coaches often scream and yell and try to make quick scores by getting their players to kick the ball back in-bounds as fast as possible. This is rarely the strategy employed at higher levels of play, however, where possession is key and players seek to make the best pass in, rather than the quickest pass in.

Kicking in to your own goalkeeper is not a bad strategy, but only if defense is not heavy toward the goal. Fortunately, the defense must allow space from the kick-in spot for you to kick the ball in. Check your league rules, but the defense is most likely required to give you three to five yards distance from the kick-in spot. Your coach can also help by sending players forward toward the opponent's goal. The defense will be forced to cover the players sent forward, possibly leaving your keeper open for the pass in. When in doubt, however, always kick toward the goal you're trying to score into. You can't actually score a goal from a kick-in, but kicking toward that goal is safer than kicking back toward your own goal if defense is heavy in the area.

You may recall in soccer that the offense surrenders possession of the ball if the player's foot comes off the ground on a throw-in. It is a coach's worst nightmare to surrender possession due to lack of concentration on throw-ins. The futsal equivalent of this rule is that the player may not step in-bounds until after they he or she has kicked the ball back in play. Similar to soccer, the kicker may not touch the ball again until it has been touched by another player. Due to the faster action of play, there will be many opportunities within a futsal game for kick-ins. There is no reason to surrender possession due to an improper kick-in, as long as the proper technique is drilled during practice.

Figure 33: Placing the Ball for a Kick-In

Corner Kick

A corner kick results when the defensive team touches the ball last before it fully crosses the end line of the goal they're defending. The kick is taken by the offensive team in the closest corner to the side of the goal where the ball crossed the line. Check your league rules, but the defense is most likely required to give you three to five yards distance from the kick in spot.

One strategy is to try to kick the ball directly in front of the goal and hope that in the ensuing mayhem one of your teammates can strike the ball into the goal. In addition to one or two interior targets, however, a far side target, and one or two outside targets should be made available. This allows for plenty of initial and rebound offensive options. Don't underestimate the potential of scoring from a corner kick.

Because of the scoring potential from corner kick situations, teams must practice defending the corner kick. The goalkeeper will likely be stationed at the near-side goal post.

Figure 34: Goalkeeper at the Goal Post to Defend a Corner Kick

Beyond that, each coach will have his or her own philosophy. Perhaps the coach builds a small four-player box roughly as wide and deep as the goal, so as to be able to respond to a ball played either toward the goal, out in front of the goal, or in the air. Perhaps a coach will position three players out in front of the goal to protect from the long shot. There is no magic formula, just make sure that your team knows how important corner kick opportunities can be, that sufficient practice time has been devoted to the situation, and that everyone is clear on their roles.

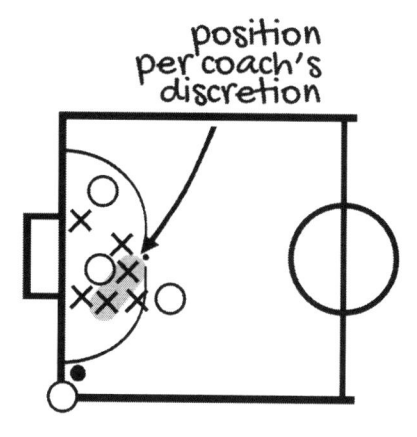

Figure 35: Corner Kick Situation

Keep in mind that everyone must know exactly what to do and be able to do it quickly, because like all other restarts in futsal, this one must occur within four seconds. It is best to be ready and in position as soon as the offensive player marks the ball in the corner and prepares to take the kick.

Goal Clearance

When a team trying to score into a goal touches the ball last before it crosses the goal line at that goal, the defending team is awarded a goal clearance. The goalkeeper has four seconds to distribute the ball by throwing or rolling it. The ball must be cleared all the way outside the penalty area (most likely the basketball three point line if playing in a gym not designed for futsal) and the keeper may not touch the ball again until another player touches it. The ball should also not be played back to the keeper until after it has crossed forward of the midcourt line.

Youth Futsal Skills and Strategies

Figure 36: Goalkeeper Distributing the Ball by Rolling with One Hand

Figure 37: Goalkeeper Distributing the Ball by Rolling with Two Hands

Figure 38: Goalkeeper Distributing the Ball by Throwing

The opposing team must leave the penalty area and no one may reenter until after the ball has crossed outside the boundaries of the penalty area. Some leagues will make rules about how long of a pass can be made, in an attempt to discourage throwing the full length of the court.

The offensive strategy should be to spread out and give the goalkeeper plenty of options, both short options and at least one longer option. The typical clearance situation will feature three players back and one player forward. A coach may send two players forward, or even three players forward, if he or she is looking for a quick score and wants to apply scoring pressure to the opposing team.

In looking for the long option, the keeper will likely want to approach the edge of the penalty area to allow for the longer throw. The goal will be left open, but the goalkeeper should have time to return to the goal, since the ball is being thrown so far away.

The goalkeeper will not step as far away from the goal on a shorter clearance. In this scenario, she or he will need to return more rapidly to cover the goal in case the ball is stolen and comes quickly sailing back toward the goal.

Free Kick

Free kicks are either direct, or indirect. The referee will signal which applies. A raised arm indicates an indirect kick. A horizontal arm indicates a direct kick. Coaches must make sure that players pay attention to the signal, know what each of the two signals means, and respond quickly to line up for the kick based on the team's previously agreed upon and practiced free kick formation.

Goals may not be scored directly from an indirect free kick since the ball must touch another player first. Direct free kicks should be aimed directly into the goal, and a goal can be scored directly from the kick. Please review the FIFA Laws of the Game for complete information on the rules regarding free kicks and when each type applies.

One approach that coaches will employ to indirect free kicks features an initial kicker at the ball, a player back behind the kicker, and a player spread out to each side as passing targets. The initial kicker will review the defensive alignment and decide what to do. She or he might initially pass to one of the side players if the defense leaves one side or the other open with their free kick defense. Alternatively, she or he might tap the ball lightly, indicating that the player stationed behind should take a running start and clobber the ball toward the goal. The initial kicker may not touch the ball again until the second kicker has touched it.

At an advanced level, the second kicker coming from behind might even be taught to read defensive movement toward the ball and learn when to pass to one of the side players rather than always clobbering the ball directly at the goal. In any scenario, the coach might designate either the kicker or the player behind the kicker to stay back after the kick in order to be ready to stop the ball should something go wrong and the opposing team come racing out with the ball.

Defensively, most coaches will choose to build a wall to protect the goal from a free kick. A wall utilizing all four court players is a rare strategy, but can be employed at the goal line, since the whole team can basically fill the width of the goal.

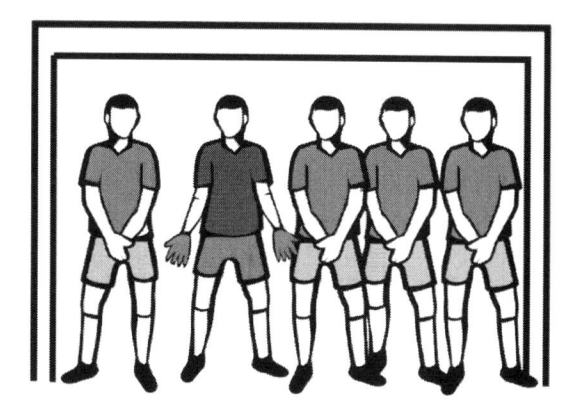

Figure 39: Everyone in the Wall

A two-player or three-player wall is more common, and can have the goalkeeper at one post and another player at the opposite post. The player at the post opposite the goalkeeper will let the players forming the wall know when they are in the right position, directly in front of him or her and aligned on a straight line from the goalpost to the ball. The goalkeeper is on the open side, allowing him or her to retain vision of the play. Everyone in the wall except the goalkeeper must be instructed not to use hands to stop the ball, but must also protect their bodies from the oncoming kick.

Figure 40: A Two-player Wall

Youth Futsal Skills and Strategies

An alternative version of the two-player wall features a field player stationed back and out to each side of the wall to protect from a kick played from either side. The goalkeeper must direct the location of the wall so that it is aligned with the goalpost and ball, then move to the opposite side to situate herself or himself to obtain a good view of the play.

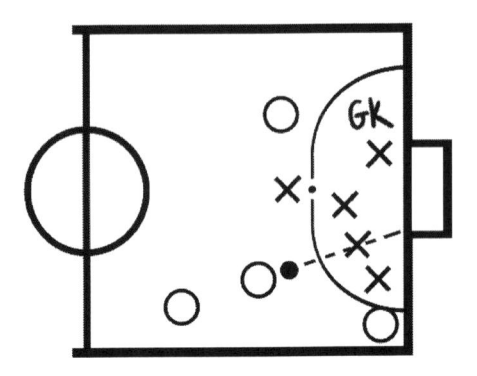

Figure 41: Free Kick Situation

In futsal, as in basketball, the number of team fouls is recorded. Once a team has more than five fouls in a half, the defensive team is no longer allowed to form a wall to block the direct free kick. After reaching the foul threshold, the kicking team is also allowed to take the kick from either the spot of the foul or the secondary penalty spot, whichever is to their advantage. This rule encourages clean, skilled play, and is meant to protect the players from over-aggression. Some youth leagues may use a number lower than five accumulated fouls as the threshold when this rule kicks in. Be sure to understand your league's rules.

Once you have reached the number of accumulated fouls, the keeper is the only line of defense. The keeper must spread wide and come out from the goal. Don't come too far out or the kicker will kick the ball right through your legs. You need to balance reaction time with angle of delivery by the kicker. Be able to drop down and defend the kick using any part of your body.

Figure 42: Goalkeeper Ready to Defend

Figure 43: Goalkeeper Dropping Down One Knee to Defend the Goal

Figure 44: Goalkeeper Dropping Down One Leg to Defend the Goal

Penalty Kick

The penalty kick only involves the ball on the penalty mark, one designated kicker, and the goalkeeper. The goalkeeper is only allowed to move back and forth along the goal line. All other players must remain outside the penalty area, and must remain a specified distance behind the penalty mark.

The penalty kick is unique to sports. It is a rare, isolated one-on-one situation within a team game. Everyone stops to watch, as the penalty kick becomes the center of attention in the gym. The penalty kick resembles a game of chess as much as it does a long-distance boxing match. Will the kicker boot the ball past the keeper into a corner of the goal, or will the keeper be able to perceive the intentions of the kicker and knock the ball out of play?

Truth be told, the kicker normally has a huge advantage, especially if the team has a powerful and accurate kicker with nerves of steel and a stoic poker face who can take the shot. Teams must be well disciplined to avoid foul situations inside the penalty area which lead to penalty kicks.

Goalkeeper Play

Believe it or not, footwork is the most important aspect of goalkeeper play. Whenever possible, goalkeepers must always get their whole body in front of the ball rather than reaching only with their arms. Like all futsal or soccer players, goalkeepers must strive to have their weight forward on the balls of the feet, rather than back on their heels in order to have quick movement in any direction.

Figure 45: Goalkeeper Getting the Whole Body in Front of the Ball

Try to reach with two hands rather than using a single hand whenever possible. Goalkeepers should be encouraged to use an underhand pattern for scooping low balls and an overhand pattern for bringing in high balls. The ball should be tucked into the chest or belly immediately upon receiving it.

Figure 46: Goalkeeper with Fingers Pointing Down Ready for a Low Ball

Figure 47: Goalkeeper with Fingers Pointing up Ready for a High Ball

Goalkeepers should practice distributing the ball by rolling or throwing. Because the court is much smaller than a soccer field, punting of the ball is not allowed in youth futsal.

Goalkeepers should have good foot skills: able to receive, dribble, and pass the ball with their feet. Goalkeepers are a valuable outlet for on-court players to pass back to in order for the team to retain possession. Most goalkeepers at high levels of play actually spend as much game time, if not more, with the ball at their feet as in their hands. Remember not to touch a ball with your hands that was played back to you by your own teammate; use your feet instead in order to avoid a penalty. Only touch balls with your hands that were kicked at you by your opponents.

As the goalkeeper, you are the last line of defense. Your on-court teammates should be taught to do everything they can to make sure that a ball played by the opponents never gets through to you; but no matter how hard they try, some balls will come your way. Just as in individual defense, the *good, better, best* strategy applies to your work as well.

In order to stop a goal, you sometimes must thump the ball out of bounds. That's *good*. Sometimes you'll boot the ball toward the opposite goal. That's *better*. If at all possible, you should try to control the ball and redistribute it to your teammates in order to regain possession. That's *best*.

Goalkeeper training should involve a stretching routine for flexibility. Players should stretch after warming up, especially focusing on the legs, hips, waist, and lower back.

Goalkeeper Strategy

The first strategic bit of advice for goalkeepers is to not stand back inside the goal; be in front of the goal. If you're inside the goal you might make a wonderful catch, but the goal has already been scored when it crossed the goal line. Also, standing a bit further out gives you the opportunity to recover a ball that might initially get beyond your own first effort to stop it.

The second bit of strategic advice is to use your allowed time in distributing the ball. Goalkeepers are allowed four seconds to dispose of

Youth Futsal Skills and Strategies

the ball after stopping a goal. Look around, find your best option, and deliver the ball safely within the allotted time. Some young athletes have a difficult time gaging how long four seconds really is. For example, there are some young basketball players who, when told there are ten seconds left in a game, will race to midcourt and heave a long shot up, leaving about eight seconds remaining in the game. Don't underestimate how long four seconds is; practice the timing.

Most importantly, be alert. Because of the short field, small number of field players to serve as obstructions, and rapid speed of gameplay, the futsal goalkeeper must always be ready for action. Teams will rapidly change from offense to defense, and back again. The goalkeeper must always be aware of changes in the game and be ready should an attacking kick come toward the goal. Just as it does for on-court players, futsal prepares soccer goalkeepers' reaction skills better than soccer itself does.

Goalkeeper Wars

The fundamental game for goalkeeper development is Goalkeeper Wars. Two goalkeepers stand in front of their goals and try to score in the other goal by rolling, bouncing, throwing, or kicking the ball toward the opposing goalkeeper. The game is played sideways across the court. Otherwise the distance between goals would be too far, and reaction time so long, that it would not be challenging. For more challenge, or with advanced keepers, the second goal can be placed at the second penalty mark instead.

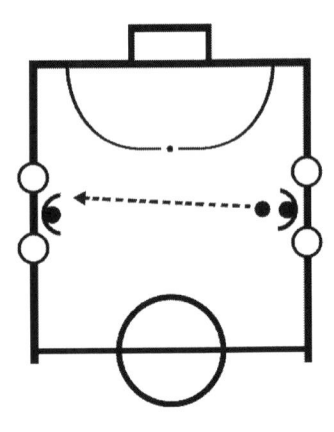

Figure 48: Goalkeeper Wars

Take it easy at first, and progress once you've determined the level of your partner. Start with some rolled balls, progress to some thrown bounced balls, and move up in difficulty from there. Even though the game is called WARS, don't send a blazing ball full speed at a partner on your first turn. You might be playing with someone that you aren't even sure is able to catch the ball. The game is less about winning by scoring goals, and more about working with your partner to help each other develop good goalkeeper technique.

Some Fun Developmental Games

Juggling

A lot of balls end up in the air in a futsal game. For that reason, the ability to control balls in the air is quite an important skill to possess. More precisely, the ability to get a ball from the air onto the floor and retain possession of it is invaluable in futsal.

Soccer and futsal players are known for their ability to control the ball using any part of their body, except the hands of course. Not only is it valuable training, but juggling is fun. Juggling involves using the top of the thigh (not the knee), the top of the foot, the inside of the foot, the outside of the foot, the forehead, and the chest.

Figure 49: Juggling with the Top of the Thigh

Youth Futsal Skills and Strategies

Figure 50: Juggling with the Top of the Foot

Figure 51: Juggling with the Inside of the Foot

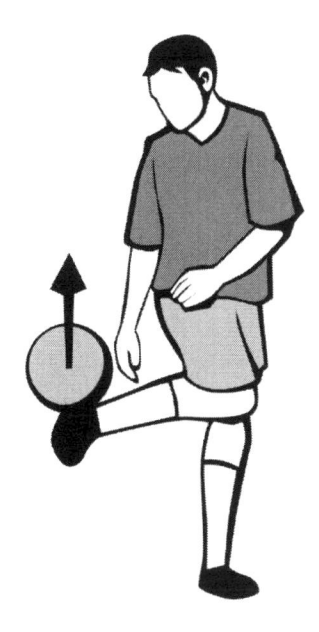

Figure 52: Juggling with the Outside of the Foot

Figure 53: Juggling with the Forehead

Figure 54: Juggling with the Chest

Begin with single bouncing. Isolate the body part you want to train. For example, say you want to learn to use the inside of the foot for juggling. Start by dropping the ball, letting it bounce off the floor, then tapping it up with the inside of the foot, and catching it with the hands. You'll quickly learn that you need to keep the inside of the foot parallel to the floor in order to make the ball bounce straight up.

Next, progress to seeing how many bounces you can do with the inside of the foot. Drop the ball, allow it to bounce off the floor, hit it with the inside of the foot, allow it to bounce off the floor, hit it with the inside of the foot, allow it to bounce off the floor, and keep going until you miss.

Finally, progress to not having the ball hit the floor in between bounces on the foot. You'll see that you need to keep the body loose and relaxed, and keep your weight up toward the front of the feet so you can move freely and quickly.

Learn to use both the right and left sides of the body. After you have mastered each body part individually, you can start combining them. You might even learn an around-the-world circuit. A sample starter around-the-world circuit would be top of right foot, inside of right foot, right thigh, left thigh, inside of left foot, top of left foot, then back again. Keep practicing, and you might even be able to add the outside of the foot, the chest, and the forehead to your around-the-world circuit. Experiment making your own around-the-world patterns.

Soccer Tennis (or Soccer Volleyball)

Soccer tennis is just what it sounds like. It can be played on a regular tennis court, or simply back and forth over a line on the gym floor if a net isn't available. Serve the ball, then keep the ball in the air, passing it back and forth over the net or line. Soccer tennis is essentially two-person juggling, in a game format.

Start close to the net, then work on moving further away as your skill increases. Don't worry about getting the ball back over the net on one touch; just don't let the ball go out of bounds or stop on the floor before sending it back across the net. You might need three of four touches to control the ball and send it back over the net. It is also acceptable to allow the ball to hit the floor before or between touches.

As you can tell, we don't worry much about rules or scoring in our version of soccer tennis. Think more about partnership, and less about winning. You're looking to increase your juggling technique, and longer rallies will meet that need better than unreturnable serves.

Soccer tennis can be played with one player per side, doubles, triples, or even larger numbers per side. Communication and teamwork is important. With teams, you are allowed to pass to your teammate before sending the ball back over the net. Older players might practice heading the ball over the net, which would simulate heading the ball into the goal in a futsal match. Players under twelve years of age, however, should be discouraged from heading the ball, due to the potential of head injury that can result at younger ages.

Four Square

A fun driveway game, futsal four square is another fun way to test your juggling prowess. If you allow the ball to stop or go out of bounds, then you move back a square. Can you make it to the king's square? How long can you stay there?

Youth Futsal Skills and Strategies

Just like soccer tennis, four square requires quick reflex movement to meet the ball. This is accomplished by keeping the weight balanced and staying on the balls of the feet rather than flat or on the heel. A soft touch, parallel to the floor, is required to control the ball and accurately place it where you want.

Sharks and Minnows

Sharks and minnows is the universal game which teaches dribbling, protection, getting free from a defender, individual defense, and partner defense. It is also a lot of fun for all ages.

Use half of a court. The minnows station themselves on one sideline. Each minnow has a ball. Select two sharks to play in the middle of the court. The minnows must dribble across the court to the other side. The sharks must recover the ball from a minnow and kick it out of bounds. Once a minnow's ball has been kicked out by a shark, that minnow leaves her or his ball aside, and becomes a shark. A minnow is also converted into a shark if he or she loses the ball without interference by the shark, such as dribbling it out of bounds without the shark touching the ball.

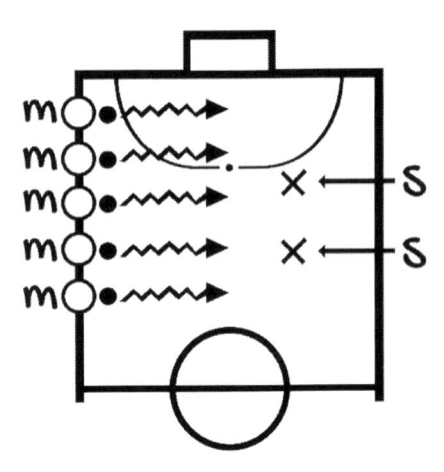

Figure 55: Sharks and Minnows

Play continues until only two minnows remain. Those two minnows become the sharks on the next round.

Another approach to the game is that only half of the minnows start with a ball. Minnows work in pairs and may pass to the partner in order to get the ball across the court. If a shark intercepts the ball, both minnow partners join the ranks of the sharks.

Coaching Responsibilities

Coaching Fundamentals

Let's begin with some general principles which apply to all youth coaches. Do not be disrespectful, or negative with your speech. Decide to be a teacher rather than a screamer.

Be positive. Praise players when they make a great decision or execute a play properly. Learn your players' names and call them by name whenever possible.

Do not punish players with laps, or pushups; instead encourage them to seek success by being motivated by your praise. At the same time, however, enforce respect, listening, and not interrupting your instructions.

Be sure to keep the line of communication open with parents. A coach should know the family situation of players, including who is allowed to pick a player up from practice. A coach should avoid being alone with a player. Do not give a player a ride to or from practice or games without someone else present. Avoid social media interaction with your players.

Avoid drills that include a lot of time standing in lines. If you're doing 1 v 1 games, consider dividing the court into two or more small courts so that as many people can be involved at one time as possible. Also, have enough balls so that everyone can have a ball at their feet during individual drills.

College students may be able to focus through a long lecture, but youth soccer players cannot. A decent guideline is that you have one second per life of the child to get your point across. With six year olds, for example, you have six seconds to spew forth your instructional wisdom. With twelve year olds, you have twelve seconds. Spend more time than that, and much of what you've said is hopelessly lost.

You've read this book; so you have a lot of knowledge to share. It is important, however, to pick the right moment to share that knowledge. The best approach is to wait until what you want to teach becomes a problem for the player, then make an appropriate suggestion at a natural break in the action.

For example, let's say you have a player who is always getting the ball stolen from them because their touch isn't soft enough and they dribble the ball out too far in front of their body. Most importantly, you must allow them to make the mistake. At a break in the action, perhaps after the opponent has stolen the ball and scored, demonstrate for them how to keep that problem from occurring again by keeping the dribble closer to their own body.

You should coach, and let the players play. You might be young and vibrant, and although it may be fun to join in the action, you'll do your best coaching from outside the play. At a break in the action, come in to demonstrate wrong and right methods. Make your final point by asking questions, allowing the players to give you the answer as to why the correct method is the better choice.

Be age appropriate with your instruction. Six and seven year olds shouldn't play positions. Instead teach them general concepts such as spread out on offense, compress on defense. Teach young players to recognize that there is someone on their team other than themselves. Any successful pass at this age should be celebrated like they've just made a last-second shot. The instructions for situations like corner kicks and free kicks for young teams should likewise be simple. Use simple instructions such as *"kick in front of the goal"*, *"build a wall"*, etc. Practicing once per week for an hour is sufficient for this age group.

Eight to ten year olds can begin learning responsibilities. There will naturally not be a lot of motion off the ball with this age range. The players will tend to be a bit more static in their approach. One player may be assigned to play back, one forward, and so forth. Every player should be allowed to play every position to try it out, even if it means losing games. Emphasize responsibilities, not position names. For example, use terms like *"last line of defense"*, *"break ahead of the pack"*, *"play wide"*, and *"control the middle"* rather than position names.

When bad things happen, point out what happens when players don't fulfil their responsibility to the team. The team's best dribbler may not enjoy playing toward the back, but if they take it upon themselves to race forward when they're assigned to play back, then there is no last line of defense. Twice per week one-hour practices is sufficient for this age group.

Usually by the time the players are eleven or twelve years old, you need to take the game up a notch and develop some plays and patterns. Your team must have a common strategy so that everyone is on the same page. For example, when the ball goes out of bounds everyone should know who sends it in. Perhaps that decision will even depend on which side the ball goes out on and whether it goes out in the backcourt or frontcourt. Much of what is written in this book applies especially well to this age group and they should be able to grasp all of the topics presented here.

When you are leading on the scoreboard, the team should know what to do. When you are behind on the scoreboard, the team should know what approach to take. Make sure everyone knows the game plan, and spend time in practice working through these situations in your 5 v 5 practice games. At this age, the focus moves from developing fundamentals to developing a feel for team strategy, being part of the team, and sacrificing for the good of the team. This age group will need twice per week 1.5-hour practices.

By age 14 and up, the plays can get more complex. There will be more movement off the ball and players can interchange roles. At this stage, the team is fluid and the parts are interchangeable as was discussed in the *4 v 4 and 5 v 5* chapter. At a recreational level, twice per week 1.5-hour practices are fine for this age group. Teams comprised of players wanting to develop for competitive levels should practice three times per week for two hours each.

Practice Organization

Coaches should be professional, disciplined, and organized. Be ready for each practice with a practice plan prepared ahead of time.

Check the court before and during practice to make safety the top priority. Make sure there are no spills, loose tiles, or faulty equipment that could lead to injury. Have your cones set up, the goals secured, your pennies organized by color, and be ready ten minutes prior to the scheduled start of practice.

Encourage your team to arrive early. This is their time for some light dribbling, passing, and shooting. Since this is the player's time, try not to interfere unless safety is possibly compromised by horseplay.

Typical Practice Plan
1. Dynamic Warm-ups
2. Individual and Partner Work
3. Fun Game
4. Small-sided Game
5. Parts of the Game
6. Goalkeeper Wars
7. 5 v 5 Game

Practice begins with dynamic warm-ups. There is no need for static stretching of a cold, tight player. The player must be warmed up before any stretching can be effective. Dynamic warm-ups lightly and safely stretch and prepare the player for increased activity.

Dynamic warm-up exercises include marching with knees high, skipping with knees high, side-to-side shuffle slides made by pushing with one leg and pulling with the other, walking with straight legs like a mummy, squats, butt kicks, and fast feet with tippy toes. Make your own dynamic warm-up or search online videos for routines.

After dynamic warm-ups, proceed into some individual work with the ball. Direct the players to practice specific dribble or juggling moves. After a few minutes, turn the individual work into partner work and practice passing and shielding drills.

A fun game follows the individual and partner ball work. Use one of the games from the *Some Fun Developmental Games* chapter.

Next, use a small-sided game to teach specific principles. A coach might begin a season by building up through 1 v 1, then 1 v 2, and then 2 v 3. After this initial three practice-session buildup, a coach can return to these small-sided games to teach whichever concept needs refinement or to practice advantage and disadvantage situations.

The next part of practice should be working with parts of the game. Notice that similar to building up the small-sided games, three practice sessions are required at the start of a season to get through all of the three aspects of the game covered in the *Parts of the Game* chapter. After these three sessions, the coach can work on whichever part of the game the coach determines needs the most improvement.

Allow some time for a game of Goalkeeper Wars; then finish with a full 5 v 5 game if number of players permit. Use your 5 v 5 time to practice the scenarios discussed in the *Game Situations* chapter, to practice holding onto a lead, and to practice coming back from a deficit.

The Game

Game time is the time to let the players play. The spotlight on the coach ended at practice; this is the time for the players to show what they've learned. Youth players will never be able to make the quick decisions needed if the coach refuses to cut the umbilical cord and is always directing the players exactly when to shoot, or exactly when and where to pass. This is not chess with live players; so don't try to direct each maneuver from the sidelines.

Youth coaches are encouraged to adopt a development focus rather than a win-at-all-costs focus. The first time in sports that winning truly counts is at the varsity level of high school, when teams are playing for regional or divisional titles. All levels prior to that should ultimately be developmental in nature. Grade your coaching by how many players sign up to play again next season rather than by how many games your team won.

Use the game as an opportunity to demonstrate good sportsmanship. Don't be afraid to recognize good plays from the opposite team.

What will you do if the opposing team shows up at the game and doesn't field enough players to play? Will you take the win via forfeit in order to stay atop the league standings? Will you loan the other team some of your players for each half so that everyone gets valuable practice playing time? The approach you take tells a lot about your focus for coaching the game.

Check your league rules to determine if a mercy rule exists. A league, for example, might issue a formal statement requesting that a team with a five goal advantage refrain from scoring again until the advantage is under five goals. The statement might even ask that you pull a player, or allow the opponent to field an extra player.

Even if your league doesn't have a mercy rule, what will your approach be if you have a dominant player? Will you keep that player in a scoring position the entire game? Will you move that player to a defensive role, or substitute them off to allow all of your players to develop?

Perhaps more telling is what does a dominant player do if they are substituted off or placed in a non-scoring role? Do they support and encourage their teammates? Take your responsibility seriously to teach important life lessons, not just futsal skills.

Players must be expected to respect others. This includes teammates, opponents, and referees. Foul language will not be tolerated. Taunting or belittling will not be tolerated. Arguing with referees will not be tolerated. After a game, the players and coach should shake hands with each of the opposing team's players, the opposing coach, and the referees.

Futsal allows substitution on the fly. Unlike basketball, the player coming off the court must be across the sideline in front of your bench before the substitute player can come on. Consider your substitution patterns and playing time for each player. Will you use four-player squads and replace everyone at once, or will you select pinpoint substitutions? Remember that the goalkeeper position is intense and must be considered in your substitution pattern. There isn't a right and wrong approach to substitutions, so develop a strategy which works for you and your team.

What will you say before a game? At halftime? During a timeout? Keeping your players ages in mind, you should be direct and to the point. Perhaps you want to emphasize defending the goal, recovering the ball, or attacking the opponent's goal. Perhaps you want to praise the effort of a particular player. Skip the lengthy motivational speech, stick to one or two points, and express your thoughts directly without flowery, metaphoric language.

Speaking of timeouts, while it is extremely comical to hear converted basketball coaches shouting *"TIME OUT! TIME OUT!"* in the distance on an outdoor soccer field, that isn't the case in futsal. As you may know, there are no timeouts in soccer, but there are in futsal. The game of futsal allows one timeout per half of play. Use them when you need to explain a critical lineup on a special play.

Similar to pre-game and in-game speeches, post-game speeches should be short and to the point. Don't spend time analyzing what just happened. It may be tough not to, considering you've spent the entire game refraining from directing each and every play. You might be ready to explode with insight, but you must refrain. You've evaluated your team's performance throughout the course of the game in order to start planning your next practice, but keep in mind that practice doesn't start right after the game. Despite your inclination to spew forth volumes of knowledge, remember that the game, even the post-game, belongs to the kids. Hold your thoughts until the start of the next practice session and instead use your post-game time to pick out a few things that the team did well and praise those aspects of the game.

Parent's Responsibilities

Parents play a crucial role in a child's athletic development. First of all, however, parents must clearly understand their role. It may seem unnecessary to state the obvious, but *the parent is not the player, the parent is not the coach, the parent is not the referee,* and *the parent is not the league manager.* The parent is the parent.

The parent is not the player: Futsal is a game of quick decisions. Players need to be taught to trust their instincts. Yelling *"SHOOT!"* and *"PASS!"* from the stands does not encourage decision-making, it encourages robot-like dependence on your instructions and inhibits players from becoming playmakers. Allow your child to play their game. Should you desire to play, there may be adult futsal leagues available in your area.

The parent is not the coach: Your child might be the best goalkeeper on her or his team. Your child might be the best scorer, or the best defender. Why is the coach playing someone else in the role that your child obviously deserves? Remember, the job of the coach is to develop every player, not just your player. Also, only those who are at every practice and within every huddle will know the philosophy that the team is taking toward a certain play. Your instruction from the stands might be in complete disagreement to what the coach has instructed. Who is your child to obey? You, or the coach? Why place your child in a position to make such a difficult decision? Alternatively, consider that league managers often have a difficult time finding the correct number of volunteers to coach youth teams. Now that you've read this book, why not consider stepping forward to volunteer to help coach your child's team next season?

The parent is not the referee: The fast pace of futsal means that some calls will be questionable, perhaps even wrong. Consider what's at stake though. This is a youth game where a higher value is placed on development than on winning. Teaching sportsmanship and proper behavior is much more crucial than getting each and every call correct. If you insist on arguing every call from the stands, then consider obtaining the training necessary to become a licensed official. You'll even get paid for your service.

The parent is not the league manager: Sure, you might be able to win every game if you get the best players on your team. It might even be tempting to make some deals behind closed doors to make sure a particular group of players is on your child's team. In the long run, however, what does it really matter? Remember, these are kids, and they're playing a game.

We've discussed the roles that parents do not fill, but what is their role? First, parents should make sure their athletes are responsible for completing homework and chores. These tasks should be elevated higher than sports, higher than electronic entertainment, and higher than other hobbies.

Rather than coaching from the stands, learn to encourage from the stands. Let your player know that you saw that great play, and also let them know everything is going to be fine even when a play didn't go the way they expected. Let your player know that your love for them is unconditional, you take as much pride in their behavior as in their accomplishments, and you will support them win or lose.

Teach your child to be a good sport. Get to know the names of the other kids on the team and also encourage those players by name from the stands. Recognize great plays from the opposing team during games as well.

Remember, winning isn't everything. In fact, too much pressure turns gifted athletes into gifted former athletes. Most players will drop out of athletics prior to their teenage years. It isn't hard to fathom that this trend could be reversed if the pressure to win, and the manipulation of a kid's game by adults, wasn't present. Do your part to keep youth sports healthy, not only physically, but emotionally as well. Similar to coaches, grade your sports parent prowess by your child's desire to sign up to play again next season rather than by how many games the team won.

Encourage fun play at home. How about some 1 v 1 in the front yard? Young athletes need to alternate structured practice with just-plain-fun practice in order to keep the sport fun. It is a game after all.

Parents must be aware of proper hydration and nutrition, because their children may not know to look out for such things. Make sure that your player is hydrated before, during, and after games and practices. A good meal a few hours before a game will provide adequate energy during the match.

What about coaching your own child? This is certainly something to consider. Will you be harder on your own child and expect more from him or her? Whether intentional or not, this is often the case. Parents who coach often go to the extreme of neglecting their own child in practice and games in an effort to not show favoritism. Face it, it is your child and everyone knows it. Be the best coach that you can be to everyone on the team, including your own children. Have fun spending time together, getting to observe them interact with other children, and allowing them to see who you really are.

Printed in Great Britain
by Amazon